A TRUE BOOK™

The North Carolina Colony

KEVIN CUNNINGHAM

Children's Press®
An Imprint of Scholastic Inc.
New York   Toronto   London   Auckland   Sydney
Mexico City   New Delhi   Hong Kong
Danbury, Connecticut

Content Consultant
Jeffrey Kaja, PhD
Associate Professor of History
California State University, Northridge

Library of Congress Cataloging-in-Publication Data

Cunningham, Kevin, 1966–
  The North Carolina colony/Kevin Cunningham.
      p. cm.—(A true book)
  Includes bibliographical references and index.
    ISBN-13: 978-0-531-25395-3 (lib. bdg.)   ISBN-13: 978-0-531-26608-3 (pbk.)
    ISBN-10: 0-531-25395-3 (lib. bdg.)   ISBN-10: 0-531-26608-7 (pbk.)
    1. North Carolina—History—Colonial period, ca. 1600–1775—Juvenile literature. I. Title. II. Series.
  F257.C86 2012
  975.6'02—dc22   2011010747

All rights reserved. Published in 2012 by Children's Press, an imprint of Scholastic Inc.
Printed in China 62
SCHOLASTIC, CHILDREN'S PRESS, A TRUE BOOK, and associated logos are trademarks and/or registered trademarks of Scholastic Inc.
1 2 3 4 5 6 7 8 9 10 R 21 20 19 18 17 16 15 14 13 12

Find the Truth!

Everything you are about to read is true *except* for one of the sentences on this page.

Which one is **TRUE**?

T or F   We know what happened to the Lost Colony.

T or F   Colonists in North Carolina had several major conflicts with each other.

Find the answers in this book.

3

Contents

**The United States
Constitutional
Convention**

THE BIG TRUTH!

North Carolina's Founding Fathers

What did these founders do after the American Revolution?....... **38**

Celebrating the end of the Revolutionary War

Runaway indentured servants from Virginia were among the early settlers of North Carolina.

A NEW DESCRIPTION OF THAT Fertile and Pleasant Province OF CAROLINA: WITH A BRIEF ACCOUNT OF ITS Discovery, Settling, AND THE GOVERNMENT Thereof to this Time.

With several Remarkable Passages of Divine Providence during my Time.

By JOHN ARCHDALE: Late Governour of the same.

LONDON.
Printed for John Wyat, at the Rose in St. Paul's Church-Yard. 1707.

Timeline of North Carolina Colony History

1500s

Native peoples inhabit present-day North Carolina.

1585

Roanoke Colony is organized.

1780

The British invade North Carolina.

1789

North Carolina approves the U.S. Constitution.

CHAPTER 1

The Native Americans

Many Native American peoples inhabited present-day North Carolina in the 1500s. Groups speaking **Algonquian** languages often lived in the eastern and coastal areas. Algonquian peoples usually lived in large family groups. These groups included grandparents, parents, and children. Their rectangle-shaped houses were made of grass mats placed over a wooden frame. Wooden walls surrounded villages. The Algonquian planted their fields nearby.

Algonquian Food

Algonquian peoples grew beans and squash with several kinds of maize (corn). They also planted tobacco for use in religious ceremonies. The men of the village hunted deer and other game in the area's thick forests. These animals provided meat. They also provided skins for clothes and antlers and bones for tools. The Algonquian fished from canoes made of hollowed-out tree trunks. They used nets and wooden traps to catch fish.

A 16th century sketch shows an Algonquin village in North Carolina.

About 80,000 Iroquois people live in North America today.

Iroquois first met European settlers in the 16th century.

The Iroquoian People

Peoples speaking Iroquoian languages competed and sometimes fought with the Algonquian. The Tuscarora was one of the largest groups. They also farmed, hunted, and fished. The Cherokee may have built as many as 200 villages along the Blue Ridge Mountains to the west. The Catawba were a separate people. They spoke a language related to peoples of the Great Plains. The region's many Native Americans would face challenges from the Europeans in the next century.

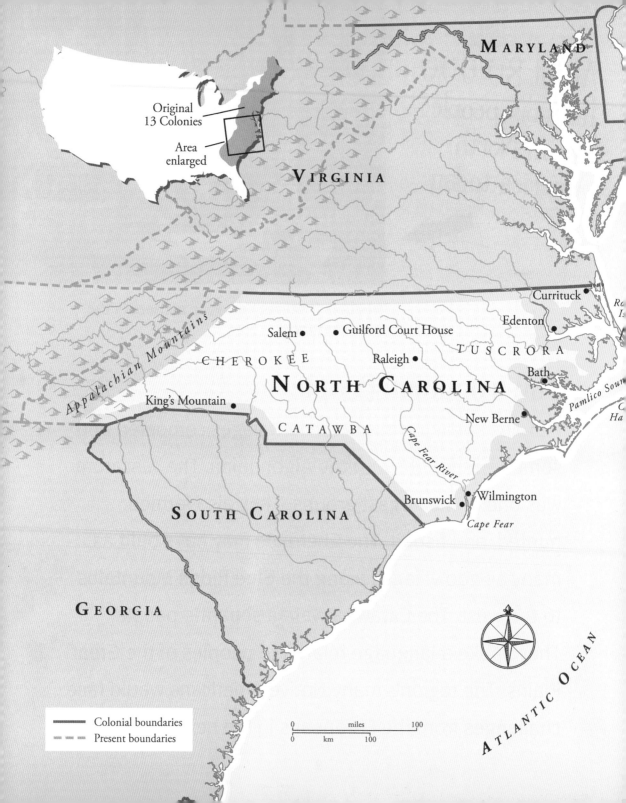

MARYLAND

Original
13 Colonies

Area
enlarged

VIRGINIA

Currituck

Edenton

Appalachian Mountains

Salem •   • Guilford Court House   TUSCRORA

CHEROKEE

Raleigh •

Bath

NORTH CAROLINA

King's Mountain •   CATAWBA   New Berne

Cape Fear River

Pamlico Sour

SOUTH CAROLINA

Brunswick   • Wilmington

Cape Fear

GEORGIA

────── Colonial boundaries
- - - - Present boundaries

| 0 | miles | 100 |
| 0 | km | 100 |

ATLANTIC OCEAN

CHAPTER 2

The Carolina Colony

European explorer Giovanni da Verrazano passed the shores of modern-day North Carolina in 1524. Spanish explorer Hernando de Soto may have entered the Appalachian Mountains around 1540 in search of gold. Two English ships sent by Sir Walter Raleigh landed at Roanoke Island in 1584. They traded with the local Native Americans. Europeans soon began to establish trading posts, settlements, and farms in the area.

Roanoke Island is only about 12 miles (19 km) long and 3 miles (5 km) wide

Fort Raleigh was the first English settlement built in North America.

Fort Raleigh

The visit by Raleigh's English ships led to the settlement of the area's first colony. One hundred male settlers built Fort Raleigh on Roanoke Island in 1585. The local Native Americans taught the Englishmen to fish and grow maize. But the settlers turned against them. The conflict led to months of fighting. The local Roanoke chief was killed. The colonists soon left Fort Raleigh on English ships.

Sir Walter Raleigh

Sir Walter Raleigh's attempts to start a colony were only a small part of the daring life he led. Raleigh was involved in plots, piracy, and soldiering. He even spent a prison term in the Tower of London. Raleigh set out on his last adventure in 1617. It was a quest to find a city of gold in South America. His men ignored his orders to avoid trouble. They attacked a Spanish fort. Raleigh was soon arrested and executed in London, so that England could avoid further trouble with Spain.

Virginia Dare was the first English baby born in North America.

John White and Virginia Dare

Raleigh assembled a second group of about 110 settlers. They put artist Fort Raleigh veteran John White in charge. The colonists landed on the Outer Banks in July 1587. They soon started building the Roanoke Colony. White's daughter Eleanor Dare gave birth to a daughter named Virginia the next month. She was the first English child born in North America. The colony soon ran short of food. White sailed for England to get supplies.

The Lost Colony

A war with Spain delayed White's return to the Roanoke Colony by almost three years. The colonists had disappeared when he returned. Not even the houses remained. White found the word *Croatoan* carved on a tree trunk. It was the name of a nearby island and native people. Bad weather prevented him from investigating the clue. The fate of the Lost Colony of Roanoke remains a mystery to this day.

John White and his men found just a single dead body on Roanoke Island.

No one knows what happened to the original Roanoke colonists.

Trying Again

The English concentrated on the Virginia colony in the early 1600s. King Charles II gave eight **proprietors** the land of today's Georgia, North Carolina, and South Carolina in 1660. They published pamphlets and newspaper articles to convince people to settle in these new colonies. But the high rents the proprietors wanted for land scared off many people. Only when the proprietors lowered the fees did settlers begin to take their offer.

The first permanent Carolina settlements were founded during the 1650s.

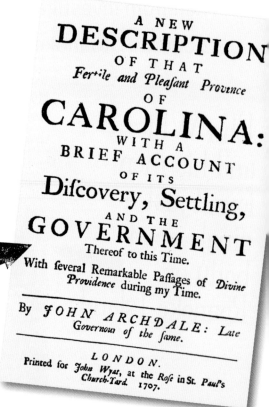

A NEW **DESCRIPTION** OF THAT Fertile and Pleasant Province OF **CAROLINA**: WITH A BRIEF ACCOUNT OF ITS Discovery, Settling, AND THE **GOVERNMENT** Thereof to this Time. With several Remarkable Passages of Divine Providence during my Time.

By *JOHN ARCHDALE*: Late Governour of the same.

LONDON. Printed for John Wyat, at the Rose in St. Paul's Church-Yard. 1707.

Life in the new colonies often involved a lot of hard work.

A New Government

The proprietors ran the Carolinas as a single colony. They wrote the Fundamental Constitutions in 1669. This established the colony's government. A governor ran the colony but took advice from a Grand Council. The colony's landowners also elected a **legislature** called an assembly. The constitutions granted religious freedom to all settlers. This was an unusual idea at the time. But the freedoms still failed to draw settlers to the northern part of Carolina.

Tobacco was an important crop for North Carolina's farmers.

It takes about four months for tobacco farmers to grow plants from seeds to harvest.

Parliament, England's legislature, added to Carolina's trouble by taxing farmers on their tobacco shipments to other colonies. Protests over the taxes led to violence between growers and the governor selected by the proprietors. Peace returned for a while. But a new law canceled the religious freedom enjoyed by Carolina settlers in 1703.

Troubled Times

The loss of religious freedom badly affected the Quakers. The Quakers were often **persecuted** for their beliefs. They managed to convince the Carolina governor to ignore the law. But worse trouble lay ahead. Two groups of armed settlers fought over religious freedom in the colony in 1711. The Tuscarora attacked settlements that same year. They had been mistreated by the colonists for years. These attacks began a two-year period of Native American assaults on villages and farms.

Colonists were sometimes forced to flee from attacking Indians.

The North Carolina **militia** and Indian **allies** defeated the Tuscarora in a bloody battle on March 25, 1713. Some Tuscarora moved to New York to live with other Iroquois peoples. But the colony faced a new problem even as the war ended in February 1715. Pirates had begun attacking Carolina's trading ships off the coast. The most famous pirate was Edward Teach. He was also known as Blackbeard. He commanded an entire fleet of ships. The authorities did not clear Carolina's waters of pirates until about 1718.

Blackbeard terrorized merchants along the coasts of Virginia and the Carolinas.

Many people told stories of Blackbeard's legendary hidden treasure for years after his death.

North Carolina began to grow more quickly after becoming a royal colony.

Royal Colony

The British government was growing impatient with North Carolina's lack of rent-paying settlers and tax-dodging farmers. It bought North Carolina from the proprietors in 1729 and turned it into a royal colony under direct control of the British government. Great Britain attempted to attract settlers by offering protection by the British army and navy. This helped boost North Carolina's population.

Many early European settlers came to North America as indentured servants.

CHAPTER 3

Everyday Life

Farming was North Carolina's main occupation. Some of the poorer farmers came to the colony as indentured servants. An indentured servant agreed to work for several years for an employer. He or she did this in return for the employer's paying the fare to North Carolina. Other farmers managed their own way to North Carolina. They bought or rented land.

Some indentured servants were given money or land once their contracts ended.

Colonial women
did the different
household tasks.

Women at Work

Farm families lived in wooden homes with a fireplace and simple handmade furniture. Women were responsible for keeping up the home and cooking. They also mended clothes and tended gardens. Families were often large. Women spent a great deal of time caring for the children. Some women also made and sold items such as clothing or candles.

Men on the Farm

Men plowed the fields and planted crops. They also brought in the crops at harvesttime. Older children and wives helped. North Carolina farmers were famous for growing tobacco. But they also produced maize, wheat, peas, and rice. Rope was made from the fiber of hemp, a tall, leafy plant. Colonists also grew flax. They spun it into linen thread to make clothing. Farmers obtained meat from livestock such as cows, horses, and pigs.

Today, North Carolina produces more tobacco than any other state.

Childhood

Children started doing chores at a young age. Older boys often worked in the fields alongside their fathers. Older girls spent time helping their mothers with work in or near the house. North Carolina had few schools. Some children learned reading and writing at home. Others did not learn it at all. Sometimes boys left home around age 12 to spend a number of years as an **apprentice** to a tradesman. They learned skills such as carpentry or barrel making.

Colonial families depended on their children to help with farmwork.

In 1729, North Carolina was home to about 6,000 slaves.

North Carolina's agriculture depended upon enslaved laborer.

Slaves

Wealthy North Carolina tobacco farmers came to rely on slave labor in the 1700s. Some enslaved people came from other colonies. But many were kidnapped in Africa and brought over on ships. Enslaved people could be beaten or sold away from their families as their owner wished. Their children also became enslaved. A very few enslaved people were able to earn enough money to buy freedom. This was done by becoming a tradesman or by growing and selling small amounts of tobacco.

The British captured the French settlement of Louisbourg during King George's War.

CHAPTER 4

Fighting for Independence

Britain, France, and Spain fought for control of North America in the 1700s. Spain attacked the Carolinas during the War of Jenkins' Ear (1739–1748) and King George's War (1744–1748). Spanish ships attacked colonial trading ships. The Spanish also raided the port of Beaufort and fought North Carolina militiamen inside Brunswick. North Carolina was soon drawn into an even bigger conflict.

 Native allies helped both sides during King George's War.

French and Indian War

Both England and France wanted the Ohio River valley. The French and Indian War began in 1754. French soldiers and their Native American allies clashed with colonial militia forces in western Pennsylvania. A crushing British defeat left North Carolina's western **frontier** open to repeated Indian attacks in 1755. Britain invaded Canada and defeated the French forces by 1760. Britain became the most powerful European country in North America.

The French and Indian War is also called the Seven Years' War.

West Versus East

The population of western regions in North Carolina grew after soldiers forced out the Cherokee from 1759 to 1761. Western settlers soon wanted to elect representatives to the legislature. But North Carolina's eastern regions controlled the legislature and kept out the westerners. A group called the Regulators was organized by residents of the western settlements. They took violent action to protest the injustice. They battled the colony's militia. The Regulators' leaders were eventually put on trial. They were found guilty and hanged.

Colonists staged protests against the new taxes.

Paying for Victory

Britain borrowed a large amount of money to pay for the war against France and for forts on the frontier. Parliament placed taxes on numerous goods in the colonies to raise funds. Colonists had paid taxes in the past. But the money had gone to the colonial governments they elected. American colonists had no representatives in Parliament to argue for their rights or defend them against taxes. Anger at "taxation without representation" grew throughout the colonies.

Sons of Liberty

The Stamp Act of 1765 forced colonists to buy a stamp to put on printed material such as newspapers and legal documents. Antitax protesters formed the Sons of Liberty. Many traders stopped bringing in British goods to sell. Parliament ended the Stamp Act and a number of other taxes they imposed. But they did not withdraw the tax they had placed on tea.

The Sons of Liberty were given their name by a member of the British Parliament.

Protests against the Stamp Act sometimes grew violent.

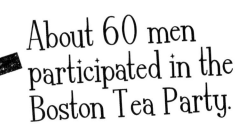

About 60 men participated in the Boston Tea Party.

The Trouble With Tea

The tea tax angered many people. Parliament made the situation even worse. It allowed a British company to sell its tea free of taxes in 1773. But it still forced American tea sellers to pay the tax. Anti-British **Patriots** protested by tossing British tea into Boston Harbor in December 1773. This event became known as the Boston Tea Party. Britain closed the harbor and stripped Massachusetts of many of its rights.

A Continental Congress met in Philadelphia in 1774. The Congress asked Britain's King George III for better treatment. Patriots in North Carolina organized committees to prepare colonists for war. The committee in Mecklenburg County declared its people free and independent. The pro-British governor of North Carolina had fled by summer. Colonists set up a new government. British troops and American militia had by then clashed west of Boston in the first battles of the American Revolutionary War.

Skilled speakers such as Patrick Henry helped convince the colonists to rebel against Great Britain.

Moore's Creek Bridge

A group of **Loyalists** tried to cross Moore's Creek Bridge on February 27, 1776. The North Carolina militiamen waiting on the other side fired with muskets and two small cannons. They killed the Loyalist leader and scattered his men. Patriots ended other Loyalist threats by arresting Loyalists across the state. North Carolina soon sent men to join George Washington's newly formed Continental army. They saw action in battles around Philadelphia in 1777.

Many men from North Carolina fought in the American Revolution.

War in the Carolinas

Britain invaded the southern colonies in 1778. In 1780, the Continentals lost a bitter fight at Charles Town, South Carolina. Capturing the city gave the British a base in the south. British general Charles Cornwallis then took control of South Carolina. Washington sent Nathanael Greene to take command of the Continental army in the south. Cornwallis headed for North Carolina. Greene split his army to trick the British into doing the same.

Nathanael Greene served in the colonial government before becoming a military officer.

North Carolina's Founding Fathers

A Second Continental Congress met in Philadelphia on May 10, 1775. Many representatives did not want to break with Britain. But pro-independence feelings grew as time passed. Representatives from 12 of the 13 colonies accepted the Declaration of Independence on July 4, 1776. New York officially accepted it on July 15th. Three North Carolina representatives signed the declaration.

Joseph Hewes

Joseph Hewes made a fortune as a New Jersey merchant before moving to North Carolina. He spoke out for independence long before most members of the Continental Congress. Hewes donated his merchant ships to the new Continental navy during the war. He used his own money to equip them.

William Hooper

William Hooper was born and educated in Boston, Massachusetts. He moved to Wilmington, North Carolina, in 1764 to practice law. He had to overcome a reputation as a Loyalist to be selected for the First Continental Congress. He became a judge after the Revolutionary War.

John Penn

John Penn was a native of Virginia. He had lived in North Carolina only a short time when he was chosen to represent the colony at the Second Continental Congress. He worked as a lawyer and government official after the war.

The Chase

Cornwallis did as Greene had hoped. Part of the British forces veered west. Cornwallis led the rest after Greene across North Carolina. A battle at Guilford Courthouse in March 1781 cost the British more than one-fourth of their men. Cornwallis marched his battered troops north to get supplies from warships off the Virginia coast. He ended up trapped by an American and French force on land and French ships offshore. His surrender on October 19 convinced Parliament to end the war.

After the war, ➡ Cornwallis became the governor of India.

Cornwallis was an experienced general in the British army.

North Carolina celebrated the end of the war, but there were hard times ahead.

The war badly damaged North Carolina's economy. The British had blocked trade for years. Many farmers and tradesmen had left their work to fight. The slow work of rebuilding America began. The new nation debated whether or not to create a national government to oversee all the states.

Onward to Statehood

Representatives from 12 states met again in Philadelphia in 1787. They planned to write a document to create a new government and put limits on that government's powers. The document was called the U.S. Constitution. It came after weeks of debate. North Carolina's leaders refused to sign it until a Bill of Rights guaranteeing a list of freedoms was included. North Carolina approved the new U.S. Constitution in November 1789. North Carolina became the 12th state of the young nation. ★

The U.S. Constitution is the oldest written constitution still in use today.

The Constitution established the U.S. government as we know it today.

True Statistics

Number of houses in a Cherokee village: 30 to 60

Number of settlers at Fort Raleigh: 100

Number of settlers at Roanoke: About 110

Year Virginia Dare was born: 1587

Number of proprietors given land in Carolina in 1660: 8

Length of service for an indentured servant: 7 years

Number of slaves in North Carolina in 1755: 19,000

Number of North Carolina signers of the Declaration of Independence: 3

Number of British troops killed and wounded at Guilford Courthouse: More than 500

Population of North Carolina in 1787: About 350,000

Did you find the truth?

F We know what happened to the Lost Colony.

T Colonists in North Carolina had several major conflicts with each other.

Resources

Books

Alex, Nan. *North Carolina*. New York: Children's Press, 2001.

Britton, Tamara L. *The North Carolina Colony*. San Diego: Checkerboard, 2001.

Fritz, Jean. *The Lost Colony of Roanoke*. New York: Putnam, 2004.

Glaser, Jason. *North Carolina*. New York: PowerKids, 2010.

Haberle, Susan E. *The North Carolina Colony*. Mankato, MN: Capstone, 2006.

Marsh, Carole. *North Carolina Native Americans*. Peachtree City, GA: Gallopade International, 2004.

Petrie, Kristin. *Sir Walter Raleigh*. San Diego: Checkerboard, 2007.

Santella, Andrew. *The Cherokee*. New York: Children's Press, 2000.

Organizations and Web Sites

Cherokee Nation

www.cherokee.org

Learn about Cherokee history and culture, and find out what's going on today on the Cherokee Reservation in Tahlequah, Oklahoma.

North Carolina State Archives

www.archives.ncdcr.gov

Look at documents and photographs that cover the history of North Carolina from its earliest days until today.

Places to Visit

Guilford Courthouse National Military Park

2332 New Garden Road
Greensboro, NC 27410
(336) 288-1776
www.nps.gov/guco
Walk the famous Revolutionary War battlefield, study the clothes and weapons used, and watch a reenactment of the battle at this site.

North Carolina Museum of History

5 East Edenton Street
Raleigh, NC 27601-1011
(919) 807-7900
www.ncmuseumofhistory.org
Learn from exhibits that tell the long history of North Carolina.

Important Words

Algonquian (al-GON-kwin)—a group of Native American peoples that once lived across eastern North America

allies (AL-eyes)—people or countries that are on the same side during a war or disagreement

apprentice (uh-PREN-tis)—a person who learns a skill by working with an expert

frontier (fruhn-TEER)—the far edge of a settled territory or country

legislature (LEJ-is-lay-chur)—a group of people who have the power to make or change laws

Loyalists (LOI-uhl-ists)—American colonists who remained faithful to Great Britain

militia (muh-LISH-uh)—a group of people who are trained to fight but who aren't professional soldiers

Patriots (PAY-tree-uhts)—American colonists opposed to Great Britain

persecuted (PUR-suh-kyoo-ted)—treated cruelly and unfairly because of one's ideas

proprietors (pro-PRI-eh-torz)—people granted ownership of a colony

Index

Page numbers in **bold** indicate illustrations

About the Author

Kevin Cunningham has written more than 40 books on disasters, the history of disease, Native Americans, and other topics. Cunningham lives near Chicago with his wife and young daughter.